Anonymous

Scotch Modesty displayed in a Series of Conversations that lately passed between an Englishman and a Scotchman

Addressed to the Worthy Patriots of England

Anonymous

**Scotch Modesty displayed in a Series of Conversations that lately passed
between an Englishman and a Scotchman**
Addressed to the Worthy Patriots of England

ISBN/EAN: 9783337307257

Printed in Europe, USA, Canada, Australia, Japan

Cover: Foto ©Suzi / pixelio.de

More available books at **www.hansebooks.com**

Scotch Modesty displayed,

IN A

SERIES of CONVERSATIONS

THAT LATELY PASSED BETWEEN

An *Englishman* and a *Scotchman*:

ADDRESSED TO THE

Worthy PATRIOTS of *England*:

And those whom His godlike predecessor would have driven from His Court, the present possessor of the throne cherishes in His bosom. Happy will it be for Him if the venomous reptiles sting him not to death. Pub. Ledger, Nᵒ 5607.

They have not only the command of this kingdom, but they are in possession of all the valuable and trusty places in the gift of the Crown. Ib. Nᵒ 5610.

Is it not sufficient that the Scots should govern this nation, and that they should destroy it's constitution, plunder it's inhabitants, occupy all places of trust and emolument? L. E. Post, Nᵒ 8712.

Considering the unjust partiality of His Majesty to a people, who never can be sincerely attached to His interest. Ib.

Every vacancy is immediately filled up by a Scotchman. Ib. Nᵒ 8731.

It would be happier for this country if it were to become a province of France, than to continue in subjection to Scottish men. Who would not sooner be a slave to a gentleman than to a blackguard?
General Advertiser, Nᵒ 427.

The SECOND EDITION.

LONDON:

Printed for JOHN BEW, Nᵒ 28, Pater Noster Row.
M,DCC,LXXVIII.

[Price 1*s.* 6*d.*]

The Reader is defired to take Notice, that the Lifts that appear in thefe Sheets were taken from the Court Kalendar for this prefent Year 1778, the new Edition, correEted to the 15th of January; and that no Changes of any Kind whatever that have been made fince that Publication, are confidered:

Worthy GENTLEMEN and BRETHREN,

THAT the many evils this poor country groans under, and that our diftreffes at home, and the difhonor and infults we meet with from abroad, were and are produced by deteftable Scotch counfels, and that, ever fince this King's acceffion to the throne, all the power in the kingdom, and all the employments of dignity, truft and profit have been lavifhly beftowed on Scotchmen, are truths fo univerfally known and felt, and fo conftantly cryed out againft in the daily papers, that it would be trifling with your attention, and a mere wafte of time, were I to fet about proving or difcanting on them with a view, Gentlemen, to your information. But I take up the pen for the fake of others; and if I addrefs myfelf to you, it is in a reafonable hope that the inftructions as well as the reproaches I mean to convey will acquire an additional weight and fanction by paffing through fo refpectable a medium. Thofe others that I mean are the Scots themfelves, our prefent tory miniftry, and their jacobite tools, and the few weak deluded people who liften to them: To thefe laft I wifh a better underftanding and better company; as to the others,

A   may

may every plague that ever galled the hearts of traitors and tyrants fall on their devoted heads!

BUT thefe bold Scots contend, that fo far from being fuch engroffers of power and places, as we reprefent them to be, they have not even that portion of influence, nor that meafure of emoluments in Great-Britain, that their numbers, their importance, and their incorporation with us by the Union Act, fhould give them an equitable claim to expect from a fair and impartial diftribution of the royal favours; and this they undertake to prove in what they call a concife and decifive manner. I fhall lay before you their allegations and arguments, as I have collected them from a feries of converfations I have lately had with one of the moft reafonable men of their country.

GENTLEMEN, fome years before we thought it effential to the peace of individuals, the honor of the nation, and it's fecurity againft foreign enemies, to infufe hatred and jealoufy into the breafts of the Southern inhabitants of this kingdom, againft thofe of the North, or, in other words, before the celebrated North-Britons came out, I had been acquainted with a Scotchman; (for you know, at that time, the Scots and we were good friends, and all national animofities had fubfided subfided and were forgotten) this man was of a decent character, with fome degree of underftanding. It would be uninterefting and tedious to tell you by what affiduities this artful perfevering Scot did lately, in a manner, force me to renew our old acquaintance, after my having induftrioufly avoided him for many years; but fo it was, he had at length the addrefs and affurance to faften upon me: he preffed me vehemently to tell him why I had kept him fo long at a diftance, at the fame time entreating me to fpeak freely, and promifing to take nothing amifs that I fhould fay.

S i r, (faid I) it is the love of my country, the refentment of it's injuries, and the feelings of an Englifhman, that have raifed my indignation againft you all. Have you not the arrangement and difpofal of every thing? Who has any rank or employment in the State, but through the influence of the Scots? Is not all the power in your hands? And who but you hold all the places of truft and profit in the kingdom? Do you not bafk and wanton in the funfhine of the court? Who robs us of the King's countenance? Who pours into his royal ear leffons of arbitrary government? And whofe counfels are liftened to but yours? Yes, you fuck the beft blood of the Kingdom, and you pocket it's treafures. And what are you all? Men born in fedition, trained up to

A 2　　　　　rebellion,

rebellion, and jacobites almoſt to a man! for
ſhame! (but ſhame is an affeaction of the mind,
unknown to a Scotchman) does not every
quarter of the town, every ſtreet ring with
our complaints; and is it not in the mouth of
every poor Engliſh Gentleman, alas! I can
get nothing, I was born on the wrong ſide of
the Tweed! Can you deny all this?

    " NoT *all*," (ſaid the Scotchman) " I ad-
" mit the laſt article, the expreſſion is pre-
" ciſely as you have ſtated it, and the cry is
" very general ; it's *truth* and *reaſonableneſs*
" will appear when I have conſidered the reſt
" of the charge,—and ſo, Sir, we hold all
" the greateſt places, and are in poſſeſſion of
" all the power in the kingdom.—Now, if
" I can diſprove that part of your poſition
" that affirms our holding the greateſt places,
" the other part of it, that imputes to us that
" enormity of power, will fall of itſelf, be-
" cauſe the one implies the other; and in as
" much as men are cut off from the firſt, by
" ſo much are they abridged of the laſt. So,
" if you pleaſe, we will contraact our diſpute,
" and join iſſue on this plain queſtion, do we
" or do we not hold the greateſt places in the
" kingdom? and this queſtion may be decided
" at once;—it affords no matter for argu-
" ment, but is a mere ſubjeact of reference.—
" The Royal Kalendar will ſettle the buſi-
" neſs,—the names of all the placemen are
                                                                               " there

" there set down ; and by knowing the name
" of each person, you can easily come to the
" knowledge of his country. However, to
" make this enquiry more commodious to
" you, I have drawn out a schedule of the
" numbers of the most exalted and conspi-
" cuous place-holders in every civil office, at
" least, every one of consequence, in the gift
" of the crown, and have distinctly marked
" the number of Scotchmen in each office.—
" I think it is correct ; but reserve to myself
" the power of correction, in case any errors
" may have escaped me through misinforma-
" tion :—look it over, compare it with the
" register from whence it is taken, and let
" me know, at our next meeting, what effect
" it hath produced in you."

LIST of the Principal Employments
in the STATE, LAW, REVENUE,
and PUBLICK OFFICES in *England.*

TREASURY. Lords Commissioners FIVE
—Secretaries TWO—Private Secretary to
the first Lord—FOUR chief Clerks—TWO
Solicitors.

Here are FOURTEEN persons, and not one
Scotch.

EXCHEQUER,

EXCHEQUER. Chancellor—Auditor—Chief Clerk—Clerk of the Debentures—Ditto of Regifters—Ditto of the Cafh-book—Ditto for making Exchequer Bills—Three Examiners of Tellers Vouchers—Clerk of the Pells—Ditto of Exitus—Ditto of Declarat—Ditto of Patents—Engroffing Clerk—Annuities under the Auditor, Two chief Clerks—Old Annuity Pells, chief Clerk—New Annuity Pells, chief Clerk—Four Tellers—Four Deputies—Tally-court, Chamberlain—Ditto—Tally-keeper of the Auditor—Clerk of the Introitus—Tally-cutter—Ufher of the Exchequer—Pay-mafters of Exchequer Bills—Ditto—Ditto—Comptroller of Exchequer Bills—Tax-office Seven Commiffioners—Impreft-office, Scotland Yard—Auditor—Deputy—Impreft-office, Lincoln's Inn—Auditor—Deputy—Auditors of the Land Revenue, &c. in fundry Counties Three—Auditor for the other Counties—Deputy—Auditor for the Principality of Wales—Deputy—Pay-mafter of Penfions—Deputy.

Here are Fifty-seven Perfons, and not one Scotch, if I am rightly informed.

High Court of CHANCERY. Lord High Chancellor—Mafter of the Rolls—Mafters in Chancery Twelve—Accomptant General—Clerk of the Crown—Deputy—Six Clerks—Record Keeper—Principal Regifter

Regifter—Lord Chancellor's Regifters Two
—Mafter of Rolls Regifters Two—Clerk
of Exceptions — Entering Regifters Two
—Clerk of Reports—Regifter of Affidavits
—Hanaper-office Mafter — Deputy—War-
den of the Fleet—Keeper of Records in the
Tower—Examiner—Three Clerks of the
Petty Bag—Two Patentees of the Sub-
pœna-office—Clerk of the Letters Patent—
Ditto of Prefentations—Patentee for Com-
miffions of Bankruptcy—Clerk of the Briefs
—Ditto of cuftody of Ideots—Principal
Secretary to the Chancellor—Secretary of
Bankrupts.

Here are FIFTY-ONE Perfons, I find no
Scotchman.

Court of KING's BENCH. Lord Chief
Juftice (N. B. appointed in the year 56)
—Three Judges—Mafter of the Crown-
office—Marfhal—Secondary—Chief Clerk
of the Rules—Chief Clerk on the Plea-fide
—Secondary—Cuftodes Brevium Two—
Clerk of the Upper Treafury—Ditto of the
Outer Treafury.

Here are FOURTEEN Perfons, Two of whom
are Scotch.

COMMON PLEAS. Chief Juftice —
Three Judges—Cuftodes Brevium FOUR
— Prothonotaries FOUR — Secondaries
THREE—

THREE — Chirographer — Secondary — Clerk of the King's Silver-office.

Here are EIGHTEEN Persons, not one Scotch.

Court of EXCHEQUER. Lord Chief Baron—THREE Barons—Curſitor Baron—Secretary to the Chancellor—Remembrancer—Firſt Secondary—Second ditto—Lord Treaſurer's Remembrancer—Firſt Secondary—Second ditto—Clerk of Errors in Exchequer Chamber—Hereditary Chief Uſher—Marſhal of Court of Exchequer—Clerk of Eſtreats—Maſter of the Office of Pleas—THREE Regiſters of Deeds.

TWENTY Perſons, no Scotchman.

PIPE OFFICE. Clerk of the Pipe—Deputy — Firſt Secondary — Second ditto — Comptroller of the Pipe.

FIVE Perſons, I believe not one of them is Scotch.

Juſtices for the Welſh Counties. Chief Juſtice —SEVEN Juſtices.

Of theſe EIGHT Perſons not one is Scotch.

Attorney General—Solicitor General.

Of theſe Two, One, namely, the laſt, is Scotch.

Dutchy

Dutchy Court of LANCASTER. Chancellor—Deputy—Attorney General—Receiver
General—Auditor of the South Parts—Ditto
of the North—Clerk of the Council.
SEVEN Perfons, not one Scotchman.

Lord PRIVY SEAL. Four Clerks.
Not one of thefe FIVE is Scotch.

SIGNET OFFICE. Four Clerks.
Not one of the FOUR is a Scot.

Secretaries of State THREE—Under Secretaries SIX—Secretary of Latin Language—
Keeper of State Papers—Collector and Tranf-
mitter of State Papers—Decypherer of Letters.
Here are THIRTEEN Perfons, I am informed
that not one of them is Scotch.

Lords Commiffioners of Trade EIGHT—
Secretary—Deputy—Solicitor and Clerk of
Reports—Counfel to the Board.
Here are TWELVE Perfons, not a Scot.

Civil Eftablifhment of AMERICA. Vice-
Admiral of all America—Auditor General
of the Plantations—Surveyor General of the
Woods—Commiffioners of Cuftoms FIVE
—Secretary—Comptroller of the Cuftoms—
Cafhier and Pay-mafter—Solicitor.
Perfons TWELVE; I imagine, from his Name
only, that One of thefe is a Scotchman.

B   CUSTOMS.

CUSTOMS. Commiffioners NINE —Se-
cretary —Comptroller General —Collector
Inwards—Ditto Outwards—Comptroller of
the Port of London—Surveyor General—
Solicitors THREE—Accomptant of Petty
Receipts—Comptroller of Iffues and Pay-
ments—Infpector General of Imports and
Exports—Regifter General of Shipping—
Infpector of Profecutions—Receiver of Fines
and Forfeitures—Chief Searcher — Deputy
—FIVE Patent Searchers—Ufher of the
Long-Room.

Here are THIRTY-TWO Perfons, not one
of them is a Scotchman.

EXCISE OFFICE. Commiffioners NINE
—Secretary—Receiver General—Comptrol-
ler of Cafh—Infpector General of Coffee,
Tea, &c.—Ditto of Brewery—Regifter to
the Commiffioners—Solicitor—Auditor of
Excife—Auditor of Hides—Comptroller of
Accounts—Deputy.

TWENTY Perfons, no Scot.

SALT OFFICE. Commiffioners FIVE—
Comptroller—Treafurer.

Perfons SEVEN, I am told that not one is
Scotch.

General POST OFFICE. Poft-mafters
General TWO—Secretary—Receiver General—Accomptant General—Infpectors of
the

the mif-fent Letters T w o—Solicitor—Refident Surveyor—Comptroller of the Inland
Office—Comptroller of the Bye Nights—
Comptroller and Refident Surveyor—Comptroller of the Foreign Office—Court Poft
(2 *l.* a day.)

FOURTEEN Perfons, I am told that not one
is Scotch.

STAMP OFFICE. Commiffioners FIVE
—Comptroller—Receiver General—Secretary.

EIGHT Perfons, no Scotchman, as I am informed.

His Majefty's MINT. Warden—Mafter and
Worker—Comptroller.

THREE Perfons, no Scot.

ADMIRALTY OFFICE. Firft Lord—
Lords Commiffioners SIx—Secretary—Deputy—Pay-mafter of Marines—Judge—Solicitor.

TWELVE Perfons, no Scot.

PAY OFFICE of the Navy. Treafurer—
Pay-mafter and Accomptant.

TWO Perfons, I believe One of them is
Scotch.

NAVY

NAVY OFFICE. Commiſſioners SEVEN —Ditto of Dock-yards THREE—Ditto at Nova Scotia.

ELEVEN Perſons, one Scotchman only, as I am told.

Surveyors General, &c. of His Majeſty's Woods in America SIX.

Of theſe SIX, I believe One is Scotch.

GREENWICH HOSPITAL. Governor —Lieutenant Governor.

Not one of theſe TWO is Scotch.

VICTUALLING OFFICE. Commiſſioners SEVEN—Secretary.

EIGHT Perſons, none Scotch.

WAR OFFICE. Secretary at War—Deputy.

Not one of theſe TWO is Scotch.

PAY OFFICE for His Majeſty's Forces. Pay-maſter General— Deputy— Caſhier— Accomptant—Ledger Keeper— Computer of off Reckonings.

SIX Perſons, no Scotchman, as I am informed.

TOWER of LONDON. Conſtable—Lieutenant Governor—Deputy—Lieutenant Governor of St. Catherine's.

Not one of theſe FOUR is Scotch.

Warden

Warden of the Cinque Ports—Lieutenant.
Two Perfons, not one of them Scotch.

CHELSEA HOSPITAL. Governor—
Lieutenant Governor—Secretary and Regif-
ter—Agent and Pay-mafter.
Four Perfons, not a Scot.

Lieutenants of Counties FIFTY-NINE.
One only is a Scotchman.

MARSHALSEA COURT. Knight Marfhal—Steward of the Court—Prothonotary.
Three Perfons, none Scotch.

Clerks of the Council Four.
Not one is Scotch.

Total of Place-holders, FOUR HUNDRED
and FIFTY-ONE, of which (errors ex-
cepted) are Scotch, only, EIGHT.

AT our next meeting, the Scotchman afked
me, if he had not " opened my eyes, and
" whether I was not *now* fatisfied, that I had
" taken up an unreafonable prejudice."

SIR, (faid I) your lift is juft as I expected
it, fallacious and defective; fallacious, in that
you

you have put down nine Commiſſioners of the Exciſe, but given us no mark by which we can find out that *one* of them is your country-man. Mr. —— is notoriouſly ſo; and it is defective, becauſe you have not put down one tenth part of the number of placemen. I ſup-poſe, that thoſe you have left out, would not have ſerved your purpoſe ſo well. Beſides you make a parade with your fifty-nine lieutenants of counties, and but one Scotchman among them. Conſider, Sir, theſe are local honors, and are, or ſhould be, held by gentlemen of conſiderable eſtates in their reſpective coun-ties. The one perſou you allude to is a Scotch nobleman, and I admit, has a very good right to the ſtation he fills, becauſe he comes with-in the diſtinction I have made; but pray don't think it a hardſhip, that other Scotchmen, who are not in the ſame predicament, ſhould not be admitted to thoſe honors.

SAWNEY was not out of countenance, nor at a loſs for an anſwer.

" SIR," (ſaid he) " the liſt is as exact as my
" care, and the information of others, would
" enable me to make it. I have purpoſely omit-
" ted ſeveral hundred places, whoſe ſalaries and
" emoluments together, do not amount to more
" than three hundred pounds a year. As to the
" number of Scotchmen that are employed, it
" is poſſible, (though I do not believe it to be
" true)

" true) that I may have been misinformed in
" a few instances; it would be absurd to sup-
" pose I intend a deceit, when detection is
" so much in your power, and so near at hand.
" If you should find any errors in that par-
" ticular, I shall congratulate you on your
" discovery; but you must find out, at least,
" two or three hundred, if you mean to give
" any colour to your assertion of our holding
" *all* the places of trust and profit.

" You are mistaken, Mr. —— was born
" in Hanover, and if his ancestors, having
" been natives of Scotland, makes him a
" Scotchman, with what propriety did our
" gracious Sovereign glory in the name of
" Briton, his ancestors having been Germans?
" —but the gentleman shall be what you please
" to make him. I deny that the list I gave
" you, is defective; it answers the purpose
" for which I drew it up, and gives you all
" that I promised. We lie under the impu-
" tation of holding all the places of trust and
" profit in the kingdom; the list shews whe-
" ther we do or not. The present King is
" calumniated for His partiality in bestowing
" them on us, whilst his late Majesty is ex-
" alted to the skies for overlooking us; both
" assumptions are equally false, and both are
" ridiculously absurd. The list shews, that
" the post of chief justice of England, is the
" only

" only capital one filled by a Scotchman; and
" in doing this, it acquits the *present* King
" of Scotch partiality in that inftance, for it's
" noble poffeffor received his appointment to
" it from the hands of the late King. It like-
" wife fhews, that the moft creditable civil
" employment held by a Scotchman, under
" the favour of His prefent Majefty, is that
" of Solicitor General, a rank inferior to that
" of a Puifne Judge, or the Premier Serjeant.
" Perhaps I may not have fet down a *tenth*
" part of the number of place-men; but in
" that omiffion I had no purpofe to ferve, but
" that of faving you and myfelf trouble. The
" fubaltern places, in offices, are ufually filled
" up by the fuperiors of them, and by mark-
" ing the country where thefe were born, I
" thought the confequence would be under-
" ftood; befides this enquiry doth not belong
" to the queftion before us, for we fuffer the
" odium of holding the places of the *greateft*
" truft and profit, not thofe of the *leaft*.
" However to fhew you, that your cavil will
" do no fervice to your caufe, even in it's
" moft extended view, I can make it appear,
" that the number of Scotchmen, in the fu-
" bordinate ftations, bears no more than a
" proportion to the appearance we make in
" the higher clafs of emoluments, and you
" have feen how ftrong we are there. In the
" Treafury-office, befides the four chief clerks,
" who are all Englifh, there are two or three
                                        " and

" and twenty others, and not one of them is
" Scotch. The War-office and Pay-office to-
" gether furnish but two; and the very ex-
" tensive office of the Customs doth not pro-
" duce a single one. The Excise furnisheth but
" one. I am not acquainted in the other of-
" fices, but am told, and indeed it appears so
" by the list of their names to which I refer
" you, and which is a good criterion, (though
" not an infallible one) by which you may
" come to the knowledge of their country.
" I say, I am told that my countrymen are very
" thinly planted in them.—Take notice, I speak
" here of the genteel employments only.

" WHAT you are pleased to say about our
" having no pretension to hold the offices of
" Lieutenants of Counties, is perfectly rea-
" sonable, but doth not apply to any thing I
" have advanced. These are stations of great
" authority and trust; and when I say that we
" have them not, I would not be understood
" to mean, that we are thereby aggrieved; for
" I avow, we have no claim to them. But
" when we are continually upbraided with
" having acquired an over-grown power, and
" the mock-patriots affect great fear, that it
" is dangerous and formidable to the State;
" surely, it is both a political and a moral
" duty to allay that fear, if it be real, or to
" expose it, if it be feigned; and the short
" and effectual way of doing this, is, first to
" fix and determine the measure of power,
" that we are in actual possession of, and then
C " to

" to fhew, that there is an infinitely greater
" one in the State, ready to outweigh and
" counteract it; and this cannot be done with-
" out entering into particulars. Sir, may I
" hope that you are fatisfied ?"

HERE he paufed for a reply, but I was not
in a humour to gratify him. He took advantage of my filence, and went on.

" I HAVE only fpoken hitherto of the civil
" employments. Let us now examine what
" power and preferments we have in the
" church, and in the military branches. As
" to the firft, I fay no more, than that there
" are twenty-fix Arch-bifhops and Bifhops,
" and that not one of them is a Scotchman.

" WHEN I confider the military line, which,
" in ftrictnefs of fpeech, confifts only of the
" fleet and army, I fhall, neverthelefs, take
" notice of the governors of provinces, towns,
" forts, &c. Some of thefe are military go-
" vernments, and others are not; but as I
" don't know where elfe to clafs them, I fhall
" take them in the groupe; after thefe I fhall
" come to the ordnance, in it's two branches,
" civil and military.

" I BEGIN firft with the army, where our
" number of officers of rank, though not fo
" large as yours, makes fo formidable an
" appearance, that it becomes me to make
" fome apology for crowding you fo much as
" we

" we do. Sir, if the fmall county of Rut-
" land were to fend out, proportionally, more
" gentlemen volunteers to the army than the
" county of Kent did, I fuppofe you would
" think it both probable and juft, that in pro-
" cefs of time Rutlandfhire would produce,
" proportionally, more officers of rank than
" Kent would. If this be reafonable, with
" refpect to the two parts of Great-Britain
" I have named, it will be fo with refpect to
" any other two parts I may name, for juftice
" is eternal and univerfal. Now Scotland has
" furnifhed a prodigious number of volun-
" teers, during the two laft wars ; many more,
" in proportion, than England hath done.
" The army and the navy take away almoft
" all our young gentlemen. The reafon is
" plain, our gentry are both poor and proud,
" (I think you will give me credit for this
" affertion) and we can neither fubmit to the
" putting our fons to trades, nor afford to
" place them in the genteeler walk of com-
" merce, nor to buy them commiffions, fo
" we fend them to fight for their bread.——
" When battles are fought, vacancies are made,
" and our lads are at hand to fill them up. It
" were the moft cruel piece of injuftice and
" impropriety, as well as an injury to the
" fervice, to refufe them commiffions, when
" they have earned them with the hazard of
" their lives, and given proof of their fpirit.
" Thus war being almoft the only profeffion

" that

" that we follow, we muſt, in courſe, pro-
" duce a great number of candidates for pre-
" ferment in that line. Theſe having gained
" their firſt object, acquire ſeniority and rank
" by perſeverance; and it is neither wonder-
" ful nor unjuſt, that ſome of them ſhould,
" at length, become general officers; and this,
" Sir, accounts for the number of them that
" appears in the army. The ſame facts and
" rule of progreſſion hold nearly in the navy.
" To this I add, that my country ſends out a
" much greater number, proportionally, of
" recruits to both branches than England
" doth; and it ſeems reaſonable, that the
" number of commiſſions granted to the
" claimants of two diſtinct parts of a king-
" dom, ſhould be in a ratio to the number of
" recruits the two parts furniſh reſpectively.
" I hope, Sir, theſe reaſons will co-operate
" in taking off part of the odium the Engliſh
" throw upon us, for ſtanding ſo much in
" their way, and in ſome degree exculpate the
" King from an unjuſt partiality to us. For,
" after all, this ſo much envied and ſo much
" cenſured goodneſs of His Majeſty to His
" Scotch officers, amounts to no more (I ſpeak
" it in all reſpect) than an act of common
" juſtice; no more than the paying the la-
" bourer his hire, and the doing that which
" he would be reprehenſible for, if he did
" not do. It is the diſpoſal of *high* places in
" offices, and at court, where little labour,
" and

" and no danger is incurred, and whence great
" honors and emoluments arife, that diftin-
" guifhes the royal bias to any particular fet
" of people. 'Till we have our *fhare*, at leaft,
" of favours in that walk, I think you might
" be filent on the fcore of partiality.

    " NOTHING now remains, but to fet be-
" fore you the numbers of Englifh and Scotch
" principal officers, as they are taken from
" the Kalendar."

Generals, Lieutenant Generals, and Major
    Generals,   -   -   -   -   146
Of which are Scotch,   -   -   -   33

Admirals, Vice-Admirals, and Rear-Admi-
    rals,   -   -   -   -   -   39
Of which are Scotch,   -   -   4

    " WE now come to the feveral Govern-
" ments, which I fhall confider with no other
" diftinction than as being at home or abroad."

Governors of places at home,   -   -   31
Of which are Scotch,   -   -   6

Governors of places abroad,   -   -   32
Of which are Scotch,   -   -   -   4

                              I have

" I have here fet down but thirty-one Go-
" vernments at home, there are in reality
" thirty-three ; but I have taken notice of the
" Tower and Cinque Ports in my former lift."

" Let us now look over the principal and
" moft lucrative employments in the Ord-
" nance, and begin with the civil branch."

Civil Branch of the ORDNANCE.

Mafter General — Lieutenant General — Sur-
veyor General — Secretary — Clerk of the
Ordnance — Treafurer and Pay - mafter —
Counfel—Secretary to the Mafter.

Among thefe there is one Scotch Gentleman,
namely, the Treafurer.

Military Branch of the ORDNANCE.

Chief Engineer and Colonel —Directors and
Lieutenant Colonels Two—Sub-Directors
and Majors Four — Comptroller of the
Laboratory— Superintendant of the Foun-
dery.

" I think you will find no Scotchman among
" thefe.

" Now, Sir, you have before you all the
" State offices, and the other principal pub-
" lick ones. You have feen in what manner
" the higheft pofts in the church are difpofed
" of,

" of, and you know how we stand in the mi-
" litary line. I here present you with a list
" of the nobility and gentry in the Royal
" houshold; read it at your leisure only;
" for the present give me credit when I in-
" form you that in that very rich and ho-
" norable assemblage we make a still more di-
" minutive figure (considering the number of
" our peers, and the claim they have to be
" distinguished at court) than in any of the
" other lists I have presented you with. On
" those I might well have rested the defence
" I have undertaken to make, from the cruel
" (and if it were not cruel, I should call it
" ridiculous) charge you have brought against
" us; but I will leave nothing untried that
" may work in you a full conviction of it's
" falsity, and bring you to a sense of shame,
" for directing the publick hatred towards us,
" on the suppofition of it's truth. Yes, Sir,
" I will vindicate our excellent King, whom
" you calumniate for acting in favour of us,
" in opposition to the principles and practice
" of His Royal Grandfather, whose venerable
" memory you perpetually wound and dif-
" grace by your insidious and hypocritical
" praises, and by making it subfervient to the
" purpofes of defamation and fedition, im-
" puting to him deeds that he never per-
" formed, and principles that he abhorred.
" In His reign, Sir, the Scotch officers shared,
" with the English, the honor of leading ar-
" mies

" mies and commanding expeditions, and the
" Englifh clamoured not at it, for the dif-
" tinction of countries was forgotten, and all
" Britons, whether born in the South or in
" the North, were confidered as countrymen
" and as O n e people, and fo we are, if the
" moft folemn compact that ever united one
" kingdom with another can make us fo.
" In that reign Lord Cathcart was at the
" head of the forces that were to have at-
" tacked Carthagena; and in that reign the
" Earl of Stair commanded the confederate
" army, at the battle of Dettingen.—Allow
" me here to make a fhort digreffion, as it
" will fhew the temper of the times *then*.—
" Immediately after that victory, the King
" thought proper to ftop the purfuit, contrary
" to the advice of the Earl, but agreeably to
" that of the Hanoverian General. When
" this news was brought over, the people
" took fire at it; their refentment (though
" perhaps too hafty, as they could not *then*
" be perfect mafters of the ftory) was natural
" and manly, and their expreffion of it was
" of a piece with the loftinefs of their
" fpirit. They did not, in a contracted,
" fpiteful and pointed manner, remark, in
" the language of the prefent times, that the
" King had affronted a Scotchman; but they
" exclaimed vehemently, that the counfel of
" a Br i t i s h General, fo eminent in his
" rank and abilities, fhould be made to give
                                        " place

" place to the fuggeftions of a foreigner.—
" But to go on : the Earl of Dunmore had
" the command of the army in Flanders, in
", the abfence of the Duke of Cumberland ;
" and the Earl of Rothes was appointed com-
" mander in chief of all the forces in Ireland.
" The Earl of Loudoun commanded in Ame-
" rica, and when that noble Peer, on account
" of fome mifunderftanding at home, was pre-
" cipitately and cruelly recalled, General
" Abercromby was vefted with the fame au-
" thority. General Sinclair had the com-
" mand of the expedition to Port l'Orient.
" Admiral Holbourn hoifted his flag on the
" American coaft, and Mr. Elliot commanded
" the armament that defeated Thurot's fqua-
" dron. Thefe appointments were all made
" in the *late* King's time. Now, Sir, is there
" any one expedition in the prefent reign,
" where a Scotchman has gone out com-
" mander in chief ? Perhaps one or two in-
" ftances may be found where the command
" has ultimately devolved on one by removal
" or refignation ; but that does not come up
" to my queftion. In the prefent unhappy
" war, which we are conftantly accufed of
" fomenting, pray what do we get ? We do
" not even come in for fifth in command.
" Two commanders in chief have been fuc-
" ceffively fent to America, and both of them
" Englifhmen ; and among the four Generals
" next in rank, not one of them has the guilt

D   " of

" of being a Scotchman. Let us now con-
" fider the naval commands :—The Eaft-
" Indies, Jamaica, the Leeward Iflands, North-
" America, Newfoundland, and the home
" ftations of Plymouth and Portfmouth,
" all thefe are filled by flag officers, but there
" is not a Scotchman among them ; and Ad-
" miral Duff, who commands in the Medi-
" teranian, is the only flag officer employed,
" whom I have the honor of calling my
" countryman.

" I fee you hear me with impatience ;
" but as you are not pleafed to vouchfafe me
" a reply, I beg for the fake of juftice that
" you will bear with me one minute longer,
" while I apply what I have faid to the quef-
" tion before us. Come, Sir, I will treat
" you with all the candor it is poffible for you
" to expect. I will not keep you to the let-
" ter of the charge, that you and the mock-
" patriots are for ever bringing againft us, of
" holding *all* the places of power and profit
" in the kingdom ; but making allowance for
" the language of party, I will fuppofe, that
" you only mean, that we hold more of them
" than the Englifh do. I can't bring your
" expreffion down lower, for a man would be
" laught at who fhould fay, that by the word
" *all* he meant the *leffer* part. If then you
" pretend that we hold the *greater* part, it
" behoves you to name fome great pofts and
" offices

" offices that I have omitted, and to shew me
" in what department that superior'ty, either
" of power or of profit, that you impute to
" us, is lodged; for if it exists, it must be
" lodged somewhere. It cannot be in foreign
" courts, for the King sends twenty-two mi-
" nisters, and only five of them are Scotch-
" men. It cannot be in the privy council,
" for that right honorable board consists of
" one hundred and three members, and there
" are but ten of them that are Scotch. Is it
" then in the cabinet? Not a Scotchman has
" a feat there. I have shewn you that it is
" not in the church, nor in the publick of-
" fices, nor in the military, nor in the court,
" nor in the country. In short it is neither
" ashore nor afloat, nor at home nor abroad.
" Where the devil then can it be? Come,
" I'll tell you where, and where only it is to
" be found.—It is lodged, Sir, with the mock-
" patriots, in the vacuums of their skulls,
" or in the hollows of their hearts."

" If I speak with indignation against those
" abominable impostors, I desire it may be
" understood that I take my aim at their cha-
" racters only, and not at their country. I
" have no inclination to reprefent the English
" as a bad people, nor could I do it with
" truth; and the only reproach I shall throw
" out against them *as a people*, in return for
" that load of unmerited abuse thrown upon

" my

" my countrymen, by the wicked and mad
" part of them, is, that the fober and vir-
" tuous part is amazingly credulous.

" CREDULITY is not a vice, but it is a
" dangerous weaknefs of the mind, that we
" fhould earneftly fet about curing, by a fre-
" quent review of the mifchief it produceth
" in fociety, and by a contemplation of that
" awful duty juftice, which, founding it's
" decrees on truths fubftantially proved, fcorns
" indolence and paffive acquiefcence, but de-
" lights in laborious inveftigation. I fay cre-
" dulity is not (in itfelf) a vice, for no one can
" control his belief, it being an involuntary
" operation of the mind, and the mind una-
" voidably acts as it is excited or moved by
" the teftimony of other men, or by the ap-
" pearance of things. It's too quick fufcep-
" tibility of *flight* impreffions, and it's pro-
" penfity to be too eafily affected by a *partial*
" and *fuperficial* view of things, (which is
" the weaknefs I fpeak of, as diftinguifhed by
" the name of credulity) arifes from an un-
" fufpecting honefty, and an habitual indo-
" lence of temper, vulgarly (though foolifhly)
" called good nature. This laft quality un-
" dermines and deftroys the good effects of
" the firft, by opening an accefs to, and as it
" were. inviting men of inventive faculties
" and bad hearts to give a *falfe* teftimony of
" facts, and throw a *counterfeit* appearance on
                                        " things,

" things, thereby vitiating the judgement,
" and drawing an unjuſt ſentence from an
" honeſt breaſt. Yes, Sir, 'tis a melancholy
" truth, that men of depraved morals often
" make the virtue of others the inſtrument
" and ſupport of their own crimes. How
" commendable, then, is that man whoſe
" *active* humanity, founded on juſtice and
" mercy, hears with pain and grief the re-
" proaches that are caſt on his neighbours,
" but hath the fortitude to make a ſtrict
" ſcrutiny into their truth, before he ſuffers
" them to take hold of his judgement, or gain
" his aſſent.

" In the queſtion before us, how eaſily
" might you have ſatisfied yourſelf of the
" truth, before you had proceeded to give
" judgement. One morning ſpent in look-
" ing over the Kalendar, would have kept
" you from the guilt of propagating the moſt
" pernicious falſities; for it is owing to the
" indolence of your temper, and not to any
" depravity of heart, that you have joined in
" the too general cry againſt the beſt of
" Kings. Sir, I perceive your ill-timed pa-
" triotic ſneer, but His Majeſty deſerves the
" epithet; and let me remind you, that a
" patriot of the firſt magnitude among you,
" (and ſorry and aſhamed am I to ſee him
" there, for, notwithſtanding ſome unaccount-
" able ſteps he hath taken, he hath virtues
" that

" that might throw a blush on the cheeks
" of the best of you) I say, this great man
" hath acknowledged Him to be so; and now
" I have quoted his authority on one occasion.
" Let me farther put you in mind, that he
" hath, in the most publick manner, with
" all the force of his masterly eloquence, re-
" probated that groundless, illiberal, (though
" fashionable) abuse of the Scots. He hath
" declared, that He made use of worthy men
" where ever He could discover them, and
" that he sought for merit in the North, and
" found it.

" HERE, Sir, I finish for this day; from
" this sample of the integrity of your leaders,
" judge what degree of credit they deserve
" in every thing else they give out. Make
" amends for your former credulity, by sus-
" pecting, for the future, whatever they shall
" advance without bringing proof, and exa-
" mine well that proof. For, remember, that
" though credulity be the child of honesty
" and good nature, it may be the parent of
" mischief and confusion."

This is the list the Scotchman put into my
hands.

LIST OF

Their MAJESTIES HOUSEHOLDS.

The KING's HOUSEHOLD.

Lord Chamberlain — Vice-Chamberlain — Secretary to Lord Chamberlain — Groom of the Stole — THIRTEEN Lords of the Bedchamber — THIRTEEN Grooms of the Bedchamber — Master of the Ceremonies — Black Rod — Master of the Robes.

Of these Three only are Scotch, *viz.* Two Lords and one Groom.

JEWEL OFFICE. The Master.

The Groom Porter — Inspector of Plays — Receiver of the Civil List Deductions.

Rangers and Keepers of Parks, Forests, &c. TWENTY-FOUR.

Of these one is Scotch.

Master of the Harriers — Master of the Buckhounds — Master of the Stag-hounds — Master Falconer.

Great WARDROBE. Keeper — Comptroller — Patent Clerk.

Lord Steward of the Household — Treasurer — Comptroller — Cofferer — Deputy Cofferer —

Master

Master of the Household—THREE Clerks
of the Green-cloth—FOUR Clerks Accoun-
tants (1080 *l. per ann.* each)—Clerk Comptroller to the Kitchen.

Yeomen of the Guard. Captain—Lieutenant.

Band of Penfioners—Captain—Lieutenant.

Master of the Horfe.

Surveyor General of the Board of Works—
Comptroller—Pay-mafter of the Works—
Surveyor of Gardens and Waters.

Lord Warden of the Stannaries — Surveyor
General—Treafurer of the Chamber-office,
and Deputy.

The QUEEN's HOUSEHOLD.

Lord Chamberlain—Vice-Chamberlain—Mif-
trefs of the Robes—SIX Ladies of the Bedchamber — SIX Maids of Honor — FIVE
Bedchamber Women—Two Keepers of the
Robes.

Treafurer—Secretary and Comptroller—Attorney General—Solicitor General—Mafter of
the Horfe.

Governor to the Prince of Wales—Preceptor
—Deputy Governor—Sub-preceptor.

Governefs

Governefs of the Royal Nurfery—Sub-gover-
nefs.

N. B. The above lift confifts only of the
moft eminent employments at court. The
number of perfons is ONE HUNDRED and
TWENTY-EIGHT, of whom FOUR are
Scotch.

GENTLEMEN, as I had never before af-
fociated with this fort of people fince my
admiffion into your fociety, I cannot but
own, that I felt myfelf ftrangely entangled.
The man's proofs feemed ftrong, but no way
reconcileable to the leffons I receive every
day from *you*. I pleafed myfelf a moment,
by thinking that this curfed Kalendar might
be under *court* management; but that idea
vanifhed when I recollected, that Mr. John
Almon, oppofite Burlington-houfe, was a pro-
prietor.—No, no, (thought I) that gentleman is no tool of miniftry!—I dreaded ex-
pofing myfelf again to the noife and fophiftry
of that talking fellow; but if I declined feeing him, he would report that I was convinced, and had given up the caufe.—I could
not bear the infamy of that imputation, for,
you know, none of us ever do that without
a valuable confideration. Well, after much
deliberation, I determined upon feeing him;

E   and

and as prudent Generals, when they are in danger of a defeat, fometimes recover the day by artfully drawing off their forces to another ground, and changing the direction of attack, fo I formed the defign to give way for the prefent, and begin my onfet in a quarter where I expected to find him unprepared. — My tormentor appeared.

Sir, (faid I) what right have you Scotchmen to any places at all in England? There are places in your own country, and as your people contribute no more than one fortieth part to the revenue of the State, I think truly that the pickings *there* will come up to your fhare of the emoluments that are gathered in the whole ifland collectively.—This was his anfwer.

" What *right have you Scotchmen to any*
" *places at all in England?* So then the af-
" fertion of our actually holding all the moft
" powerful and profitable ones in the king-
" dom is given up. It is no longer infifted on
" that we *do hold them,* but an apology is im-
" plied in your queftion for our *not holding them,*
" namely, that we have no right to them. But
" if we neither have the right, nor the poffef-
" fion, what is it you complain of? And now
" muft that bold affertion, fo continually en-
" forced, and fo rooted in the memory and be-
" lief of millions of people, fhrink in the hour
" of trial! That firft article in the mock-pa-
" triots'

" triot's creed, that darling topic, that hath so
" long ferved to impeach the King's juftice, and
" to make us the mark for the keeneft fhafts of
" malice and envy, be done away by a bare in-
" fpection into two or three lifts ? And muft you
" fuffer ill-bred facts to ftare you in the face,
" call your leaders liars and calumniators, and
" throw confufion on the countenance of thofe
" who have been fo credulous and indolent as
" to make *them* the keepers of their con-
" fciences ? Yes, Sir, you muft endure all
" this ; for a ftrong enemy ftands in your
" way, whom you hate even more than you
" do a Scotchman. I mean TRUTH!—glar-
" ing, palpable, unaffailable demonftration.

" AND now the corner ftone of your edi-
" fice being crumbled to duft, you think to
" take refuge in a little idle queftion, that
" anfwers itfelf. Yes, Sir, we have a right
" to places in England, and fo have you to
" places in Scotland, and you avail yourfelves
" of that right too : For inftance, one of the
" Barons of our Exchequer is an Englifhman,
" fo are two out of our four Commiffioners
" of the Cuftoms, as is likewife the Secretary
" of that board. I might go on, but it were
" fuperfluous, becaufe I admit, that, in ge-
" neral, the Scotch places are filled by Scotch-
" men ; and certainly, if the Englifh and we
" were to be confidered as two people, (as we
" were before the Union) we fhould have no

E 2   " pretenfions

" pretenfions to be taken care of in England;
" but fince the two kingdoms have been, by
" their own confent, confolidated into one,
" the power of the crown remaining as it
" was before that coalition, the King may
" beftow places where he pleafes without
" any regard to the points of the compafs.——
" However, as it is generally more convenient
" and defirable that gentlemen fhould enjoy
" employments in the neighbourhood of their
" eftates, houfes, and relations, it hath been
" ufual, in favour of us both, to confer them
" with an eye to that intention (with fome
" exceptions, however, as you have feen.)
" But this intention of arrangement can only
" take place with regard to thofe offices in
" Scotland that exifted antecedent to the
" Union, and have been kept up there to this
" day, becaufe many others that exifted there
" formerly were, in confequence of that me-
" morable event, annihilated with refpect to
" their locality, and abforbed in others ana-
" logous to them in England; particularly
" all offices under the Great Seal. This cir-
" cumftance would have turned many Scotch
" gentlemen adrift, if they had not been per-
" mitted to follow preferment as it travelled
" from their country to yours; and to gain
" appointments in thofe offices that had fwal-
" lowed up their own.

" I do not afk you if this reafoning be juft,
" becaufe I will not put you to the pain of ac-
" knowledging,

" knowledging, that any thing is so that fa-
" v urs the rights of a Scotchman. But I
" may afk you, if you can think it possible,
" th.t our nobility and gentry could have
" been brought to consent to a measure, that
" was for ever to bar themselves and their
" relations fr m a participation of the King's
" presence and favours, and to preclude them
" from those employments of dignity and
" emolument, that may be looked upon as
" the birth-right of some, and the reward
" of merit and services to others; I say,
" would they have proscribed their own chil-
" dren? If you are at a loss to answer this
" question, pray explain the meaning of the
" fourth article of that treaty, viz. *There shall
" be a communication of all rights and privi-
" ledges between the subjects of both kingdoms,
" except where it is otherwise agreed.* In short,
" if it was understood at that time, that we
" were to give up so many of our employ-
" ments in Scotland, and receive none in
" lieu of them in England, I can't help ob-
" serving, that the Act of Union was strangely
" miscalled; it's title should have been an Act
" of Disunion.

" When you pretend, that we contribute
" but one fortieth part to the support of the
" government, I suppose you misunderstand
" (for you certainly mistate) the fact. It is
" settled by the ninth article of the Union
                                        " Act,

" Act, that, *when England raises two millions*
" *by a Land-tax, Scotland shall raise forty-eight*
" *thousand pounds:* — Call this the fortieth part.
" Now by the eighteenth article it is enacted,
" that *the laws relating to trade, customs, and the*
" *excise, shall be the same in Scotland as in Eng-*
" *land.* These imposts raise upon an average
" nine millions ; so that we are favoured in
" an article that brings in two millions, and
" assessed *equally* with yourselves in an article
" of nine millions, and this you are instructed
" to say, is paying only one fortieth part of
" the *whole.* Yet this absurdity goes down
" with the rest that are brought against
" us !"

Gentlemen, I need not point out to
you, who read every thing that concerns the
publick welfare with such intense applica-
tion and shrewdness, that my Scotchman had
begun to raise his tone and had taken up a
kind of taunting stile. I was resolved to take
him down. Come, come (said I) don't dwell
too much upon the great figure you make in
the publick supplies. It is well known you
all smuggle when you can ; for as to buying
things in a fair way, though your pride might
push you on, your penury would keep you off.
To be sure poor England would starve, if it
were not for the *Scotch* duties !

" 'Tis

" 'Tis pleasant enough (quoth he) to hear
" an Englishman talk of smuggling !

" *Loripedem rectus derideat, Æthiopem albus.*"

" And I dare say you never do it yourselves,
" but (like us) when *you can*. As to our pe-
" nury, we can no more help that crime than
" we can that other of being Scotchmen, yet
" you take infinite pleasure in reproaching us
" with both. Indeed you make us some
" amends as to the first charge, by forgetting
" yourselves sometimes, and intimating that
" we are mighty rich; and how should we be
" otherwise, when we have for so many years
" *plundered your inhabitants*, and possessed *all the*
" *valuable places in the gift of the crown! These*
" circumstances, joined to a *third* crime, *œcono-*
" *my*, which you spend so much excellent wit
" in abusing us for, must have made us rich
" indeed ! Well then ; which of these two
" opposite charges do you wish me to plead
" guilty to ? Why, as it suits your *present*
" purpose, let it be poverty. Now, Sir, if
" we are so poor, that but few of us can pur-
" chase wine, or rum, or sugars, or other ar-
" ticles the duties upon which make up the
" bulk of the revenue, still we must be ame-
" nable to those duties if ever we shall be-
" come rich, and shall actually purchase the
" articles. One part of a country is said to
" be equally taxed with another, when the
" inhabitants

" inhabitants of both, who buy like commo-
" dities, are forced to pay the fame duties
" for them.   I Suppofe there are many large
" tracts in England, where French wines and
" rum are never tafted, yet it would be ftrange
" doctrine for any man to advance, that the
" inhabitants are to be looked upon as aliens,
" and lofe their confequence and priviledges,
" becaufe they can't afford to drink claret, or
" treat their friends with rum punch."

HERE my gentleman made a full ftop---but
'twas to no effect, fo he went on again.

" MY friend (faid he) I find that you are
" again troubled with the dumb fpirit; but
" if you are not deaf too, you may hear fome-
" thing that may inform you.   In our firft
" day's converfation you was pleafed to afk
" me who poured into the Royal ear leffons
" of arbitrary government; by which quef-
" tion, I fuppofe, you meant to intimate,
" that thofe of us who are not Jacobites, are,
" at leaft, Tories.   As I can do the bufinefs in
" a few words, I will let you into the real
" ftate of parties in Scotland.   I know of only
" two parties there, namely, Whigs and Jaco-
" bites.—Tories and Republicans we have
" none:—As to the laft I do not find that we
" ftand accufed, (we fhould find more favour
" among your friends, if we did.)—You are
" ftartled at my affirming that we have no
" Tories;

" Tories; but your inftructors having kept
" that matter from your knowledge is no ar-
" gument that my pofition is falfe, but rather
" a prefumption in favour of it's truth. Shall
" I tell you why they call us Tories? The
" imputation of Jacobitifm would have ferved
" their turn as well, but it would have been
" too grofs to have called us all fo, feeing fo
" many of us have fought and died in the
" caufe of the Houfe of Hanover; but as they
" were determined that not a man of us fhould
" efcape the publick hatred, they ftigmatifed
" thofe to whom they could not impute Ja-
" cobitifm, with the odious name of Tories,
" a character than which nothing can be more
" heterogeneous and repugnant to our genius,
" education and prejudices. No, Sir, we have
" no faith in the indefefible hereditary right of
" Kings, nor in their divine right, nor in
" paffive obedience and non-refiftance in mat-
" ters where religion is to be rooted up, or
" the laws laid wafte; thefe doctrines may
" have been broached in England, but they
" have never croffed the Tweed; and I will
" be bold to fay, that if the Jacobites that
" were among us had gained their point, and
" placed their idol on the throne, they never
" would have been Tories to him. Turn
" over the hiftories of every part of the globe,
" and you will not find a country that hath
" exerted itfelf with that unrelenting uncon-
" quered fpirit againft tyrants and arbitrary

F   " power

" power that ours hath done at all times, and
" on all occasions. It is not my bufinefs to
" read hiftory to you, and if you are igno-
" rant, no doubt you will be obftinate; but
" your leaders know (I don't fay they will
" own it) that what I advance is true. One
" gentieman, however, has had the candor to
" own it, and I quote him with pleafure, be-
" caufe I never heard that he has been fuf-
" pected of partiality to my countrymen, I
" mean the author of the North Briton. After
" affirming that the Scotch nation has always
" regarded the Houfe of Stuart in the true
" light, (*i. e.* as tyrants and cowards) he fays,
" *the hiftory of Scotland fhews how little that*
" *nation is difpofed to fubmit to oppreffions* AT
" HOME;" and he then goes on to prove it from
" other authority. See North Briton, No. 36.
" I cannot help remarking here (by the by)
" how very erroneous, though common, is
" that afperfion of our being infolent in office,
" and fawning to thofe who are ranked above
" us.—The very reverfe of this is true.—The
" authorities I have juft quoted fhew us to be
" a people that are not likely to be over pa-
" tient under *perfonal* indignities; and I may
" make my appeal to the character of every
" officer I have mentioned, as having had a
" command under the late King, for a refu-
" tation of any charge that imputes to us a
" haughty over-bearing carriage in office.

" WELL

" WELL, I said that the Scots are either
" Whigs or Jacobites ; but as the word Whig
" hath, from time to time, had many diffe-
" rent fignifications impofed upon it, fo that
" it is now become uninteligible, I muft
" tell you what fpecies of Whigifm diftin-
" guifhes us. We are not of that fort that,
" during the reign of King William, joined
" with the Tories (though they hated them)
" in always oppofing his meafures ; they had
" too much of Republicanifm, Anarchy, or
" private views in their complexion ; nor do
" we come up to the perfection of the men
" who now affume that title. What are we
" then ? We are friends to the revolution,
" friends to the reigning family, and friends
" to the conftitution as it *now* ftands ; in fhort
" we are that kind of Whigs that conftituted
" the *old* miniftry in Queen Anne's reign, who
" had a folid and rational love for the people,
" and in confequence of that love thought,
" that loyalty and fubordination were duties
" that ought to be inculcated as the only hu-
" man means of making them happy and fafe ;
" and though they abhorred paffive obedience
" and non-refiftance, as applied to the dia-
" bolical purpofes above-mentioned, yet they
" did not mean to erafe loyalty and obedience
" out of the catalogue of focial virtues, and
" replace them by their oppofite vices difo-
" bedience and fedition, as a fet of men who
" dare call themfelves Whigs now do.—If

" they

" they only called themfelves patriots, I fhould
" not be offended. Patriotifm is a complex
" idea, that involves and combines many ca-
" pital virtues; and when they with their low
" paffions and vices pretend to it, the plea-
" fantry of the image amufes me. Their pa-
" trionifm (mind I fay *their*) agrees exactly
" with Locke's diffinition of wit, which (fays
" his abridger, for I have not read Locke thefe
" many years) confifts moft in the affemblage
" of ideas, and putting thofe together with
" quicknefs and variety which have the leaft
" refemblance to form agreeable vifions. But
" when thefe men call themfelves Whigs,
" they ought, at leaft, to bate one of their
" charges againft us, and never henceforth
" talk of *Scotch* impudence.

" O u r prefent Whigs (for they perfift in
" keeping up that title) are playing the fame
" game that the oppofition did in the reigns
" of King William and Queen Anne; they
" pitied, flattered, courted, and betrayed the
" people; told them they were cheated, abufed,
" that their blood was fpilt in fruitlefs expe-
" ditions, and their treafure wafted to enrich
" minifters, with all that kind of tragical cant
" that you now read every day in the papers.
" The people believed them, yes, the people
" who are always in the right, and whofe
" voice is the voice of God. What was the
" confequence ? a King who had reftored their
" conftitution,

" conſtitution, and was the bulwark of their
" religion, became hated, inſulted, and felt
" every mark of popular oppoſition and in-
" gratitude. And in Queen Anne's reign this
" ſame Majeſty of the people ſet it's face a-
" gainſt the wiſeſt and beſt miniſtry that ever
" diffuſed ſtrength and brilliancy on a king-
" dom, expelled them, and brought in a ſet
" of men, whoſe firſt efforts were to change
" the ſucceſſion, after having already made
" Great-Britain a by-word to all the nations
" in the world for perfidy and treachery to
" it's allies. If you aſk of what party deno-
" mination theſe oppoſitions were, I anſwer
" that the firſt was almoſt of every party ;
" diſcontented Whigs, biggoted Tories, Ja-
" cobites, Republicans, Levellers, Papiſts,
" Preſbetyrians, and half a ſcore other ſects
" with their ſub-diviſions, who, though they
" deteſted and envied each other, juſt as the
" members of the preſent oppoſition do, yet
" (like the preſent) joined all their forces to
" form one GLORIOUS OPPOSITION, as
" they called theirs, and as you like them
" call yours. In Queen Anne's reign the peo-
" ple, indeed, were taught to be Tories, as
" that character ſuited beſt with the Queen's
" humor, but their leaders were in their
" hearts of different ſects. Harley, afterwards
" Earl of Oxford, the chief of them, was
" bred a Preſbetyrian, and was one of the four
" Whigs who had oppoſed King William.

" As

" As the mock-patriots boaft fo much of
" the love and good opinion of the people, I
" hope I have not ftrayed out of my road in
" fhewing you how little the merits of men,
" and the value of things is to be eftimated
" by popular opinion. Nothing is more eafily
" obtained (provided you will fet afide the
" honeft man and take up the hypocrite) nor
" more hard to keep. In POLITICAL MAT-
" TERS the people may be tuned to any thing;
" and that fame credulity and good-nature
" that makes them *to-day* the inftruments for
" one fet of men to play upon, may *to-morrow*
" leave them open to the practice of another
" fet, who have more fkill or fortune to hit
" the right key of flattery and condolence.

" I intimated juft now that the word Whig
" had been fo ftrained and ftretched beyond
" it's firft fignification, that now it conveys
" no pofitive diftinct idea to the mind of what
" it is. I repeat it: I know men of fourfcore
" years of age, who had been trained up in
" Whig principles, connected themfelves all
" their lives with that party, who had always
" called themfelves Whigs, were reputed to
" be fo, and received as fuch. Men, who
" had grown grey in the defence of the Whig
" doctrine, and now, behold, thefe men have
" all along miftaken their own character, and
" the world has been deceived in them! they
" are Tories! for they maintain that honor and
" obedience

" obedience is due to the King, they have a
" sacred reverence for parliaments, and they
" think that respect belongs to magistracy.

" In my attempt to bring the word Whig
" back to it's true meaning, and restore the
" character to it's lustre, I was under the ne-
" cessity of wiping away every stain that hath
" been thrown upon it. Let this, Sir, be my
" apology for striking out the pretensions of
" your friends to that denomination. I doubt
" not but in a little time, when the world shall
" be convinced of your incompetency to stand
" in the rank of Whigs, you yourselves will
" hit off some title that may go down with
" the people :—Indeed it is almost time that
" you should.—The word Patriot too cannot
" hold out much longer; it's meaning begins
" to be understood. Why should you not call
" yourselves the Godly, or Christ's Saints?
" Other men of the same stamp with *many* of
" you, and with the *same object* in view, for-
" merly did so with amazing success.

" I have taken the pains to analise your
" whole complicated mass of opposition, and,
" upon separating it's parts, I find that, if
" from that medley of characters that consti-
" tuted the opposition in King William's
" reign, you take away the Papists, Jacobites,
" and Tories (for I would not charge you with
" more than you deserve, or I can prove) and
" fill

" fill their feats with R — ck —— mites,
" S—lb—nites, and Place-hunters; you will
" take in all thofe men who, led by fome po-
" litical principle or other, would overturn
" the government for the good of the people;
" all thofe who, having no attention to the
" people, are under the influence of partial
" connections and friendfhips; and all thofe
" who, difregarding both general and parti-
" cular interefts, extend their views no far-
" ther than to the filling their own pockets.
" —But ftill their are two characters wanting
" to compleat the prefent hodge podge of Pa-
" triotifm : The firft of thefe confifts of men
" who have, or think they have, received fome
" injury or flight; thefe are wound up and
" put in motion by pique and refentment *only*,
" and are callous to every fentiment that doth
" not arife from revenge, or that doth not tend
" to the feeding it.—I hope thefe are few;
" but fome of them are of the firft rank in
" the kingdom, and are too dextrous and
" powerful in all the variegated arts of mif-
" chief.—The laft fet of oppofers I am to
" fpeak to are thofe who are merely and avow-
" edly fo for oppofition's fake. How often
" have I feen a pompous coxcomb take the
" lead in a company and exclaim, God forbid
" that there fhould be no oppofition in this
" country! if ever that fnould happen we are
" an undone people!—Obferve, I underftand
" the word oppofition *here* to be a conftant
                              " indifcriminate

" indiscriminate one; for if it be taken only
" as an occasional and just one to those mea-
" sures that are bad, I have nothing to speak
" to, for the sentiment is unexceptionable;
" but it is so very evident, that I think that
" the men who usher it in with so much so-
" lemnity have a deeper and more extended
" meaning. If, then, it be understood that
" there should always exist a set of men who
" are *constantly* to oppose administration, I
" pronounce that the position is dangerous,
" and the more so, on account of a plausibility
" that is it's passport to a pretty general re-
" ception; but, in reality, it is no more than
" one of those high sounding sentiments that
" wants but to be developed to make it de-
" tested and exploded. I wish I had leisure
" to expose it in all it's views, and trace it in
" all it's consequences.—Take, however, a
" remark or two; Support, and opposition are
" relative terms, and commendable or other-
" wise, according to the subjects they are
" connected with; therefore opposition can-
" not *always* be right, unless measures should
" always be wrong, which is a case not easy
" to be conceived.—The supporting bad mea-
" sures is not a whit more atrocious than the
" opposing good ones; and those men who
" resolve to defend every one, and those who
" are as determined to tilt at them all, equally
" expose themselves to the obloquy of making
" a sacrifice of truth and propriety to injustice

G   " and

" and a rotten policy.—No man is juftifiable
" in obftructing the meafures of adminiftra-
" tion, unlefs it be in matters that he is qua-
" lified to underftand, and if he doth not un-
" derftand them (I care not how unpopular
" the fentiment may be, I am fure common
" fenfe is on my fide) he ought to be filent.
" If his avocations or his lazinefs have barred
" his knowledge on any particular topic, let
" him, at leaft, keep up a defent referve, and
" a manly pride, and not let himfelf down to
" the ftation of a poft-boy, who is not an-
" fwerable for the intelligence he carries, or
" to the office of a fpeaking trumpet, that
" fpeaks by the breath of others."

HERE, Gentlemen, I took occafion to obferve to my Scotchman that he had got into
the beaten track of minifterial agents, who
are mighty induftrious in recommending it to
the people to fhut their eyes, and their ears,
and their mouths.—Yes, yes, (faid I) if you
could bring that about, you might mould us
to what you pleafe, and enflave us all; but
this leffon will not go down in a country of
liberty, and, Sir, let me tell you, it is the
duty of every honeft man to be a watchman
for the State, and to give the people timely
notice of every danger, left they find it out
when it is too late, and fink under it.—You
have fpent much time in giving me advice,
and in abufing my friends. I have heard you

with

with great patience; but you really bear me down with a torrent of words.—Who told you that *many* in the oppofition are Republicans and Levellers? and on what ground do you infinuate that they have dark defigns?— You call us calumniators, whilft you yourfelf are acting the part of a railer and defamer. I mention not this with a view that you fhould anfwer it, for I grow weary of the fubject; but to fhew you that I fee into your ftratagem. You are raifing a duft, that under the cover of it, you may fteal away from a charge which you cannot bear up againft. Why do you elude my pofition that this country is governed by Scotch counfels? for you do but trifle, when you tell me that your countrymen do not occupy the ftations that give an *official* and *oftenfible* accefs to the King's clofet. 'Tis known that they find their way to it by fome *fecret* paffages, particularly two of your noblemen, I need not name them; and it is more dangerous, certainly more fufpicious, that they fhould convey their fentiments in whifpers, than if they delivered them at a board.—Befides you have not yet acquitted your people of being, moft of them, Jacobites. If you mean to converfe with me any longer, fpeak to thefe points, and don't continue dodging and fharking from the main queftions; and when you have done this, throw back your attention to the years fifteen and forty-five, and try if all your arts and fhifts can abfolve

or

or palliate the behaviour of your countrymen at those times; and then tell me, fairly, if the memory of your paft rebellions doth not give us juft caufe to entertain fears and jealoufies about you.

It was wonderful, my friends, to fee with what ferenity and compofure the Scotchman heard all this. His countenance raifed in me the idea of that dignity of character expreffed by the MENS SIBI CONSCIA RECTI. Yet though he feemed quite eafy under my reproaches, and perfectly prepared with an anfwer, I will do him the juftice to own that there appeared no air of triumph or infolence in him.—All this might be art! he thus went on.

" SIR, I am ready to admit that you have
" heard me with patience, and am not with-
" out hope that a time may come when you
" will find your account in having done fo;
" if I have been tedious in fome places, and
" have feemed to keep too long from the main
" points, it was not from any unwillingnefs
" to return to them, but from the method of
" the defence I am engaged in, which muft
" be accommodated to the nature of the
" charge.—Now to fupport this charge, no
" fact or proof is adduced; it is merely in-
" vention improved into hear-fay. What mode
" of defence then could be fo fitting as that
" of

" of laying open the political characters of
" it's fabricators and promulgers? This I
" have done, and it is with you to determine
" whether their principles and publick con-
" duct entitle them to a degree of credit suf-
" ficient to overturn the authorities I have
" produced.—*Who told me that many in the*
" *opposition are Republicans and Levellers?* In-
" deed, Sir, you are a weak advocate for your
" friends, if you deny it; they avow it them-
" selves; their doctrines speak it; but lest
" these should not speak plain enough, their
" writers take up the signatures of Cromwell,
" Fairfax, Ireton, Bradshaw, Milton, Pym,
" and others of that kidney. Doth this want
" a comment? and are these used casually and
" without a meaning?—and *on what ground*
" *do I insinuate* (by the by I do more than in-
" sinuate it) *that they have dark designs?* This
" is my reason; when any particular minister
" is the object, the writer, after calling up
" the people against him, and using every art
" that can exalt popular madness into frenzy,
" and carry zeal into action, piously admo-
" nishes him to take care of his soul, that the
" vengeance of Heaven is at hand, and will
" be sudden and unexpected: The writers in
" this way sign Felton.—A curious Epitaph
" to the honorable memory of Mr. President
" Bradshaw lately came out; and verses have
" appeared commendatory of a celebrated af-
" sassin; I have not the paper by me, and if
                              " I mutilate

" I mutilate the text, I afk the author's par-
" don, but I think the laft line runs thus :

Who ftrikes a Tyrant, ftrikes for human kind.

" I am not deep enough read in Englifh poe-
" try to know whether it be original or a
" quotation, but I have wit enough to under-
" ftand it's tendency ; and what think you of
" thefe that were written fome years ago ?

—— ——— — *May every Villiers feel*
The keen deep fearchings of a Felton's fteel.

" So now you know what you have to do
" when you are offended with any particular
" minifter ; only intimate to fome enthufiaf-
" tick follower of your's, that he is as dan-
" gerous a man as George Villiers Duke of
" Buckingham was, and you may chance to
" fee *poetical* juftice executed upon him.—
" Some Felton may do it for *the honor of*
" *God, and good of his country.* I have
" heard too of an odd expreffion, about town,
" of de Witting a minifter ; but I hope this was
" only the conceit of fome drunken porter at
" an ale houfe ; it could not come from a
" man of fafhion or humanity. Good God,
" if this fcheme of affaffinations fhould take
" place, where will it end !—Well, Sir, have
" have I made good my charge ?

" You

" You miftake me ftrangely, Sir, I wifh,
" I exhort the people to *open their eyes and*
" *their ears,* and every avenue to their under-
" ftandings ; and then, but not 'till then, to
" *open their mouths too :* For how can a man
" inform me, if he hath not informed him-
" felf ? By all means let them watch over the
" State, but let them qualify themfelves firft
" to be watchmen before they undertake to
" perform the office. The poor fellow who
" proclaims to the parifh the hour of the
" night, and the appearance of the weather,
" firft liftens to the clock, and looks at the
" fky ; but if he neglected to make ufe of his
" fenfes, and, like you, proclaimed at ran-
" dom, we, his worfhipful mafters, would
" foon difmifs him, as one whofe roaring and
" bawling ferved only to difturb and deceive
" us. It vexes me when I fee rational beings,
" free agents, arranged and pofted like walls
" and pillars only to raife a multiple echo.

" I do not believe that the two Scotch no-
" blemen you allude to get fecret accefs, and
" deal in whifpers in the manner you repre-
" fent : You have afferted it, and it lies with
" you to prove it.—If you alledge that the
" bufinefs is of too private a nature to admit
" of proof, I muft fay, then, that you are
" performing the part of a mifchievous bufy
" prattler, in afferting any thing injurious to
" private characters, that you cannot fupport.
But

" But let us look into the probability of
" this matter; one of thefe noble perfons is
" wholly taken up in works of literature and
" philofophy, hath conceived an invincible
" difguft to politicks, and is feldom in town.
" The other attends the duty of his high of-
" fice, and the parliament, with too much
" affiduity, and, in his leifure hours, the
" chearful focial turn of his mind engages
" him too much in rational friendly converfe,
" to leave him either time or tafte for enter-
" ing into private cabals.—You don't know
" the men you are talking of; and I am a-
" fhamed to employ my time in anfwering
" private fcandal; but I have one argu-
" ment that ought to be irrefragable with
" your friends, as it is drawn from one of
" their own favourite principles, I mean the
" little care they take of us their countrymen,
" when they might eafily provide for many of
" us, if they had the King fo much in their
" power as is pretended; fo that you are
" brought to this dilemma, you muft either
" withdraw your pofition, or acquit them of
" nationality, a crime, it feems, in a Scotch-
" man, and a virtue in an Englifhman.—If
" the King condefcends to profefs a regard
" for thefe noblemen, His Majefty doth no
" more than act in common with every honeft
" man who knows them. THEY will not
" *fling him to death.* If they had ever repro-
" bated a meafure in publick which they had,
                                        " filently,

" filently, fuffered to pafs in council, or had
" ever carried the fecrets of the King to a
" leader of an oppofition, they might juftly
" have been thought capable of fuch a deed,
" and would have given too much colour to
" their enemies to confider them as *venemous*
" *reptiles*, to ufe another expreffion of an ele-
" gant writer of your's.

 " I come now to fpeak of the Jacobites
" that are among us. Indeed you do them
" too much honor to mention them. A few
" bed-ridden men and women, who cannot
" fhake off their old prejudices, make up al-
" moft the whole corps. The field of Cullo-
" den, and your fcaffolds and gibbets in Eng-
" land have provided for the greateft number
" that lived in the year forty-five ; fome ef-
" caped to France, and fome eluded the long
" and ftrict fearch that was made by the
" King's forces; thefe, when juftice had been
" nearly fatisfied, and when keeping the fword
" of punifhment longer unfheathed, might
" have favoured of unrelenting feverity (which
" was far from being the character of the late
" King) came from their coverts, and, join-
" ing with the few who had been pardoned,
" enlifted in the army; and together with
" great numbers taken out of thofe clans that
" had retained their loyalty, and were the
" moft numerous, formed very confiderable
" reinforcements to the troops in America
   H   " and

" and Germany, where they are reported to
" have done their duty.—I intimated that the
" loyal clans were the moſt numerous. If I
" am guilty of a miſreprcſentation, I ſubject
" myſelf to detection, by giving you the par-
" ticulars, as they have been delivered to me.
" On the King's ſide were the Campbells,
" M'Clouds, Monroes, M'Kays, Sutherlands,
" Grants, and two regiments of lowlanders,
" raiſed at Edinburgh and Glaſgow. The
" rebel clans were the Mackintoſhes, Frazers,
" M'Pherſons, M'Donalds of Glangary, Mac-
" kenzies (a part only), and a regiment of
" lowlanders, led by Lord Lewis Gordon.
" You will find, upon enquiry, that the for-
" mer were in general the ſtrongeſt bodies of
" men.

    " B u t what gave the finiſhing blow to Ja-
" cobitiſm in Scotland, was that wife mea-
" ſure that took place and paſſed into a law ;
" I mean that of aboliſhing the power of the
" heads of clans, and thereby dealing out to
" the highlanders the bleſſing of freedom, in
" common with all their fellow-ſubjects in
" Great-Britain. This excellent Act, as it
" endeared the Government to them, com-
" pleated a reformation in their politicks, and
" opened a large ſource of ſtrength and credit
" to the whole kingdom ; So that when peo-
" ple talk *now* of the Jacobites in Scotland,
" as a party that can diſturb the State, they
                                              " are

" are either ignorant of what they talk about,
" or have defigns that are not quite innocent.

" B u t I have detained you long, and will,
" therefore, defer to our next meeting what
" I have to fay, in relation to the behaviour
" of the Scots, in the years fifteen and forty-
" five, which you queftion me about, but
" which, having paffed fo long ago, and there
" being fo few alive that were concerned in
" either, I think you might have forborn to
" mention; but as you deduce from the me-
" mory of thofe tranfactions a reafon for keep-
" ing a jealous eye over us *now*, I find myfelf
" under a neceffity of fpeaking to them. I
" fhall then undertake to fhew that your fears
" (if you really have any) are without foun-
" dation; perhaps I may go a ftep farther,
" and make it appear that your reproaches
" *now* are ill-timed, unprovoked, wanton and
" cruel. When this bufinefs fhall be gone
" through, I fhall congratulate you on being
" in fight of land, for I fhall only further
" throw in your way two or three remarks that
" arife from the whole of our converfation,
" which I have as much reafon, at leaft, as
" you to be weary of, for I have received no
" inftruction by it, and, if it is not your own
" fault, you have."

Gentlemen,

Gentlemen, it was not long before the Scotchman and I met again, when he revived the subject, by saying,

" At our last meeting you called upon me
" to vindicate the behaviour of the Scots, at
" the two points of time you then specified.
" If I were disposed to enter upon the defence
" of what was done in the year fifteen, I
" should make you my debtor for pleading the
" cause of *your* countrymen, as well as that
" of my own, for the crime was common.
" If you did not bring so many men into the
" field as we did, it was not owing to a want
" of courage or inclination, for at that time
" great numbers of you most devoutly wished
" for the return of the abdicated family. But,
" to gratify that wish, difficulties and ob-
" structions stood in your way, which the na-
" ture of our constitution and customs ex-
" empted us from:—In matters of political
" zeal there is usually but a short space be-
" tween a design and it's execution if the
" vigilance and power of the established go-
" vernment do not interpose to keep them at
" a distance.—Now the power of our chief-
" tains was at that time so enormous, that it
" superseded all magistracy, and bid defiance
" to all process of law; they could, in a few
" hours, call out all their vassals and lead
" them to action without a necessity of mak-
" ing them privy to their design.—Secrecy
" and

" and expedition are the effence of confpi-
" racies.—But the cafe was different in Eng-
" land, every man to be employed *there* muft
" be firft confulted, and his confent obtained;
" whilft the Lieutenants of counties (who
" hold their places at the will of the crown)
" and the civil officers had their rule of con-
" duct fo plainly marked out to them by the
" common courfe of law, and by orders from
" the Secretaries of State, that they could, in
" many inftances, prevent people from com-
" ing together, and fecure thofe whom they
" had caufe to fufpect; and accordingly many
" were taken up. This accounts for your de-
" bility in the execution, but doth not take
" away from the turpitude of the defign.

" IN the rebellion of forty-five the Englifh
" are not to be reproached, for I fcorn to take
" advantage of the rifing of a few ; do I ad-
" mit then that it was a Scotch rebellion ?—
" Very far from it, if you mean a *general* one,
" not a tweifth part of the peerage was con-
" cerned in it, which appeared after the un-
" common pains taken to enquire who were,
" and not a fingle minifter of the Kirk ; few
" of the lowlanders took up arms, and thefe
" were oppofed by a fuperior number, who
" drew up on the King's fide : This rebellion
" confifted of fome highland clans, and thefe
" were more than counterbalanced by the
" loyal ones: If thefe laft had been permitted

" to

" to rife fooner, which Archibald Duke of
" Argyle, and the Marquis of Tweedale ftre-
" nuoufly advifed, though by a fatal error in
" in miniftry they were not attended to, the
" rebellion would have been quafhed in it's
" infancy.—But even the highlanders who
" fought for the Pretender, are not to be con-
" fidered *individually* as Jacobites ; they knew
" no political principle, but that of a blind
" obedience and prefcriptive fidelity to their
" leaders. So that, all things confidered, there
" remain none to be apologifed for but thofe
" leaders and a few others, who, under a
" State of free agency joined them.—You
" challenge me to excufe thefe, I decline it,
" I have nothing to offer, but I take not an
" inhuman joy in aggravating their offence.
" —They paid the forfeit of their lives.—Let
" the memory of the crime perifh with it's
" perpetrators.—But your friends think other-
" wife, they give life to it, they call it up
" for malicious purpofes; they firft endeavour
" to fix the character of univerfality on what
" was very limited and partial, and then from
" that feigned and fuppofitious generality,
" draw unfair confequences, and extend them
" beyond what would follow from the pre-
" mifes, even if they were true. If you al-
" ledge that there were many of the Scots
" who wifhed well to the caufe, though they
" did not affift in it, I anfwer, perhaps it
" might be fo ; but would you execrate men
" for

" for their speculations ? None but the actors
" are rebels ; for rebellion is an action, not a
" passion : But this objection is best answered
" by a matter of fact, which is that very many
" more wished well to the King's cause,
" though they likewise did not assist in it ;
" indeed there was not time to raise and dis-
" cipline them, for when an active enemy is
" in the field, it is too late to raise recruits
" and form soldiers, they must be met with
" by those that are at hand.

    " B u t I must not yet have done with this
" idea of speculative Jacobites, because I see
" why you have recourse to it, and carry it so
" far. The absurdity of deducing a genera-
" lity of principle in a million and half of
" people, from the actions of ten thousand,
" which is the utmost that is pretended to have
" been in arms, and two thirds of them in a
" state of servitude to their chiefs, would have
" been laught at, so you break open the ca-
" binet of mens secret thoughts, which hav-
" ing garbled and adulterated to your purpose,
" you deal out as their opinions, to fill up
" the measure of your charge, and give an
" appearance of generality to an odious ap-
" pellation you chuse to insult us with.—But
" this not all. You make use of this inde-
" cent and preposterous misrepresentation of
" us as if it were a truth ; and you infer
" from it, (for that is your object) that if
                                 " most

"most of us were Jacobites in the year forty-five, we must necessarily be so now. But why so? Are there no instances of a people having changed their political principles, and taken up quite contrary ones, in a less space of time than three and thirty years? I will carry you back but a little way into the history of your own country, to shew you that it is no new thing.

"In the reign of Charles the Second the people were twice Tories and once Whigs; in the beginning of it, unconditional and unbounded loyalty was the prevailing passion, the people were Tories in the most eminent degree; (that term and it's opposite were not then invented, but I use them *here* to distinguish the principles) but the bad conduct of that prince, and the fear of a popish successor, soon gave their minds another bias. Opposition took place, and then first the Whigs set up. These were good men and meant well, but unfortunately they took into their association a set of furious Republicans, who disgraced the whole tribe, and at length sickened the people with their plots, their perjuries and their barbarities. Then again the Tories triumphed, and so great and general was the disgust against the other party, that it even superseded their fears of popery, and the name of Whig became infamous, and few kings have died more popularly bewailed

"than

" than Charles the fecond.—Such was the
" temper of the nation when James the fe-
" cond afcended the throne; that mad bigot
" foon turned the current ; the whole frame
" of legal fecurity tottered to it's foundation,
" and popery poured in like a torrent. Op-
" pofition became neceffary, meritorious, and
" univerfal ; and the doctrine of paffive obe-
" dience and non-refiftance was given up by
" it's late warmeft fupporters. A well-timed
" and juft revolution reftored religion and
" law. William was a great and an honeft
" man, but his referve and ungraceful de-
" portment created him enemies ; untoward
" circumftances gave thefe an advantage, and
" the high church men, who perhaps thought
" they had not been enough rewarded for the
" facrifice they had made of their principles,
" joined in cabals ; fome with a view only to
" diftract and perplex his meafures, and others
" to feat his rival on the throne. When
" Queen Anne came to the crown, fhe found
" the kingdom torn to pieces by factions;
" but her miniftry were fo happily chofen,
" that they nearly brought about a coalition
" of parties : Some of them had been mode-
" rate Tories, and the Whigs that were
" among them had preferved themfelves un-
" tainted with republicanifm ; their high
" underftanding and calmnefs of temper
" brought them to be well acquainted with
" each other ; and it was *then* found out that

I   " a mo-

" a moderate Tory and a moderate Whig,
" when they came to define their principles,
" were nearly the fame thing : they therefore
" joined in adopting this laft title ; and the
" people (the majority I mean) again became
" Whigs.   Never was in England fo glorious
" a combination of TRUE PATRIOTS.   Ne-
" ver did the kingdom fhine forth with fuch
" luftre ; and never were people fo happy.
" But this bright period lafted only a few
" years, and gave place to a mortifying
" change : the Queen had not great fkill in
" ftate affairs ; there is reafon to think her
" heart was good ; but fhe had not the qua-
" lities of an heroine ; and it is not to be
" marveled at, that, when the dear objects of
" conjugal and maternal tendernefs were re-
" moved, her affections fhould revert to the
" houfe from whence fhe fprang : her *new*
" favourites cherifhed this partiality ; their
" arts, as you have heard before, together
" with the Queen's moft engaging deport-
" ment, wrought upon an unguarded, good-
" natured people to clofe in with her defigns.
" The bulk of them again became violent
" Tories ; and they carried their principles
" to fuch an excefs, that it is extremely pro-
" bable, that, if her death had not happened
" at fo critical a time as it did, popery and
" defpotifm had again overwhelmed thefe
" kingdoms.

" IF

" If thefe facts are ftated with the fidelity
" and precifion I have endeavoured at, they
" will teach you how delufive is your con-
" clufion, when you infer that if we were,
" moft of us, Jacobites in the year forty-five,
" we muft neceffarily be fo at this time; for
" you cannot perfift in that wild notion,
" when you reflect on the fluctuating ftate of
" parties, but more particularly on the con-
" fequences of the victory at Culloden, and
" on the act that abolifhed clanfhip.

" But why hate, fpurn, and infult us, for
" a crime committed fo long ago? Surely the
" blood that was fpilt on that occafion was
" fufficient to wafh away the ftain. I do
" not fay that the feverity was exceffive, but
" there was no great defect of it. The act
" that paffed for trying men in England for
" crimes they had committed in Scotland, was
" going as far as it was poffible to come at
" their lives, and feemed to be a perverfion
" of the intent and liberality of the law,
" which means to lay open to every man's
" view the utmoft extent of the danger he
" incurs if he commits a crime, that the hor-
" ror of the profpect may work upon his
" fear, and make him ftop in time: the mi-
" ferable objects I am fpeaking of had not
" that advantage; they acted under the faith
" and protection of a law which enfured to
" them the right of being tried in their own

" country.

" country.—They were deceived; a *new* act
" of parliament *ex poſt faƈto* ſtarted up, and
" expoſed them to a *new* danger, which, if
" they had foreknown, perhaps the terror of
" it might have kept ſome of them innocent.
" I pretend not to dive into the political ex-
" pediency of that meaſure—it might be ne-
" ceſſary—but I contend that the ſufferers had
" a hardſhip put upon them—they had not
" fair play.—If you will, you may call me a
" Jacobite for ſaying this, I cannot help it ;
" but what I mean is to put you in mind that
" there was not ſuch a degree of lenity ſhewn
" upon that occaſion, as to make it at all ne-
" ceſſary to fill up any deficiency of puniſh-
" ment by inſults and reproaches, which, as
" far as they relate to the guilty and the pu-
" niſhed, are *now* ſuperfluous and ungenerous,
" and in as much as they are levelled indiſ-
" criminately at my countrymen, are mali-
" cious and falſe, as hath been abundantly
" proved.

" How then can you juſtify your treat-
" ment of us?—But I will bring this matter
" ſtill more home to your juſtice, your com-
" mon ſenſe, and your humanity: I will uſe
" an argument that the moſt ſubtile of your
" leaders cannot anſwer, and dare not evade :
" I ſay, then, that even ſuppoſing the rebel-
" lion to have been more general than I have
" repreſented it, and ſuppoſing too that it had
" not

" not been fufficiently punifhed, yet (and here
" will I reft my caufe) IT HATH BEEN
" FORGIVEN. The generous George the
" Second gave a receipt in full, by cherifh-
" ing us in common with the reft of his fub-
" jects, by trufting, by employing us.—He
" had no caufe to repent it ; we have ever
" fince that time manifefted a fteady loyalty ;
" we have been peaceable and dutiful at home,
" and we have gone out with chearfulnefs and
" alacrity to revenge his wrongs, and to fight
" his battles.

  " AND fhall an offence pardoned, and a-
" toned by an after conduct that hath even
" given luftre to Royal mercy, by ftamping
" it with the feal of wifdom and forefight,
" fhall that offence be called up *now* againft
" us ? *now*, when time, that fhould bury all
" injuries, and foften all refentments, hath
" lent it's healing hand, and joined itfelf to
" every other argument for a general ob-
" livion ?

  " OUR converfations now draw to an end.
" I have demonftrated, that the Scots do not
" poffefs that immenfity of power and places
" that the mock-patriots pretend : from the
" procefs of that demonftration arofe this co-
" rollary, namely, that we have not even *our*
" *fhare* of them,—I have fhewn you that fo
" far from infufing into the King notions of
                              " arbitrary

" arbitrary power, we deteſt and always have
" oppofed ſuch doctrine.—I have particula-
" rifed to you that fort of people that was en-
" gaged in the rebellion, in the year forty-
" five; and in doing that, I have made it ap-
" pear that the imputation of it's being a *na-*
" *tional* one is unjuſt and falfe.—I have then
" argued, that the offence ought to have been
" purged away by the *late* King's pardon ;
" more efpecially when every mode of com-
" penſation that natural juſtice and municipal
" rigour could require at the hands of the
" *guilty,* have been complied with ; and every
" duty that moral obligation can lay upon de-
" linquents as expiatory of their offences, hath
" been practifed, to the full, by a people,
" the bulk of whom had not been guilty of
" any offence that ſtood in need of any expia-
" tion at all.

" I ſhould grudge the time I have ſpent
" in elucidating thefe matters, if I had not
" a glimmering of hope, that my pains
" would not be entirely thrown away ; they
" are all directed to one point, namely, that
" of making peace between us. If juſtice,
" and the propriety of things have not their
" due weight with you, by being counteracted
" by the mifchievous induſtry of your leaders,
" liſten, at leaſt, to the voice of common in-
" tereſt and fafety. Great-Britain is threat-
" ned ; Never did a body require the ufe of
" all it's limbs more than this empire now
" calls for concord and harmony in all it's
" parts ;

" parts; yet these—shall I call them men, or
" monsters? persist *even now* to disjoin us.
" How can we assist you with that social affec-
" tion, and that chearfulness of spirit that
" gives energy to every blow, and sets up ho-
" nor in opposition to despair, when you are
" every day calling us traitors, and grudging
" us the very commissions that are given us to
" fight in your cause?—When I assure you,
" as I now do, that the Scots have nothing
" more at heart than to live amicably with
" the English, I think I venture upon no more
" than our very long and patient suffering un-
" der such sharp provocations and indignities
" evinces. This forbearance of ours shews,
" likewise, that we know how to distinguish
" between the natural genuine temper of a
" people, when left to themselves, and their
" adopted principles, *adopted* from men as
" much inferior to them in honesty and ge-
" nerosity, as they are their masters in craft
" and mischief. It is against *these only*, these
" mock-patriots, these leaders of yours, (and
" I believe there are not more than an
" hundred or two in the kingdom) that we
" have any resentment; and if in the course
" of our conversation I have not always
" pointed out this distinction, it was omitted
" only through impetuosity, or to avoid mul-
" tiplicity of words. This being understood,
" what remains for me before I take my
" leave? Nothing, but to exhort you to be
" just

" juſt to yourſelves, and then you will do *us*
" juſtice.—Emancipate yourſelves from that
" thraldom that your too eaſy belief and in-
" dolence have drawn you into—have opi-
" nions of your OWN.—Shall men be led in
" a ſtring? and will you give up the nobleſt
" prerogative of humanity, that of thinking
" and reaſoning, and reſt your faith upon the
" intelligence of others, (ſuch others too!)
" and decide upon it? Will you dance when
" *they* pipe, and fetch and carry at *their* bid-
" ding?

" I know it doth not come within the
" compaſs of every body to ſtudy the hiſtory
" of his own country; but it is amazing that
" men who have it in their power to come at
" this kind of knowledge ſhould ſo ſhame-
" fully neglect it's purſuit. It is the remark
" of an ingenious foreigner, that the Engliſh
" are the moſt enlightened people in the
" world in every thing but their own hiſtory.
" —He was in the right.—I wiſh men would
" ſtudy it well; it would lead them into
" drawing compariſons that would turn to
" account both in quieting their own minds
" and making them good ſubjects. Then
" would they ſee that there never was a
" time when liberty was enjoyed to the ex-
" tent it now is; that there never reigned in
" England a king, from whom any deſign of
" encroaching on it was ſo little to be feared
" as from His preſent Majeſty.—When your
" *republican*

" *republican* leaders blazon forth all the glo-
" ries of the nation under the commonwealth,
" they keep from your view that tribunal
" called the HIGH COURT OF JUSTICE,
" where men were capitally convicted with-
" out JURIES; (read the State Trials)
" not a word is said of those petty ty-
" rants the MAJOR GENERALS who
" were appointed to the government of coun-
" ties, nor of the total bar to every avenue to
" the PRESS.—They know all this, but they
" trust to your ignorance, and they are not
" deceived. They know too that the time I
" am speaking of teemed with more barba-
" rity, illegality, and insecurity to individuals,
" than ever disgraced this country, even under
" the reigns of the Stuarts or the Tudors.

" AN inspection into the merits of former
" reigns would teach you to reverence the
" present one. Then would you blush to see
" your King defamed and ridiculed, to see
" male gossops carry tittle-tattle up and down,
" and bandy tales, as void of truth as their
" authors are of common sense!

" AND now, my friend, to convince you
" how much I wish to bring you to a juster
" way of thinking, and to shew you that I
" fear not that all I have said will stand the
" test of your cooler reflection, and the scru-
" tiny of your friends, I will send you upon

K   " paper

" paper the whole of our converfation; I can
" eafily recollect all I have faid, and *your* re-
" plies will not burthen any man's memory.
" Take only this caution; when I have ftated
" any thing in a *general* way, I expect to be
" underftood *generally*; for example, when I
" ufe thefe expreffions, *the people, my country-*
" *men, we, us,* or the like, you are not to
" arraign my veracity in what I fay concern-
" ing them. becaufe you may find out *fome*
" exceptions. to the univerfality of my pofi-
" tions.—And now I bid you farewell."

WELL, Gentlemen, the Scotchman was as
good as his word; he fent me the writing,
and I think it is pretty exact. I am fenfible
how fmall a figure I have made in the contro-
verfy, but I had rather ftand before you in the
light of a weak difputant, than permit our
caufe to fuffer from fuch doctrines as he hath
advanced, if they fhould remain unanfwered.
I recommend this to your confideration, and
hope you will take him in hand.

I am, GENTLEMEN,

Your moft devoted fervant and
faithful adherent.

N. B. *The noble perfon alluded to in pages* 29 *and*
30, *and fpoken of there as living, died after thefe*
fheets were fent to the prefs.

www.ingramcontent.com/pod-product-compliance
Lightning Source LLC
Chambersburg PA
CBHW020337090426
42735CB00009B/1572